The Buddha and the Bodhi Tree

Retold by Owen Cole and Judith Lowndes
Illustrated by Tony Morris

Heinemann Educational Publishers
Halley Court, Jordan Hill, Oxford OX2 8EJ

MADRID ATHENS PARIS
FLORENCE PRAGUE WARSAW
PORTSMOUTH NH CHICAGO SAO PAULO
SINGAPORE TOKYO MELBOURNE AUCKLAND
IBADAN GABORONE JOHANNESBURG

First published 1995

95 96 97 98 99 10 9 8 7 6 5 4 3 2 1

British Library Cataloguing in Publication Data
A catalogue record for this book is available from the British Library

Starter Pack
1 of each of 12 titles: ISBN 0 435 01066 2

Library Hardback Edition
The Buddha and the Bodhi Tree: ISBN 0 431 07762 2
1 of each of 12 titles: ISBN 0 431 07763 0

Designed by Sue Vaudin; printed and bound in Hong Kong

Acknowledgements
Back cover photograph:
Ann & Bury Peerless

A long time ago a wonderful
prince was born.
He was called Siddhartha.
The little prince lived in a
palace with his father.

Everyone loved Siddhartha.
His father was very proud of him.
The palace seemed to shine because of the prince.

A wise man lived in the mountains.

He went to visit the palace.

He wanted to see little Siddhartha.

When the man saw Siddhartha he said,
"This prince will be great.
If he *stays* in the palace
he will be a wonderful king."

He said, "If the prince *leaves*
the palace he will be very important.
He will teach people to feel at peace.
Many people will listen to him.
But he will be very poor."

Siddhartha's father was sad.
"What if Siddhartha leaves the palace?" he said.
"I do not want him to go away.
I do not want him to be poor."

So Siddhartha's father looked after
him well in the palace.
He told Siddhartha how to be a
good and kind king.
Siddhartha had a very happy life.

When Siddhartha grew up he
married a lovely princess.
The prince and princess were very happy.
They lived in the palace.

“I am so lucky,” said Siddhartha.

“I have a lovely wife.

I live in a beautiful palace.

I have fun all the time.”

One day Prince Siddhartha went for a ride outside the palace.
He saw some things he had never seen before.

Siddhartha saw a man who was very ill.

This made him sad.

"I did not know that people get ill," he said.

Prince Siddhartha saw a man who was old.
The man could not walk very well.
Siddhartha was very sad.
"I did not know that people get old," he said.

Then he saw another man.

This man was dead.

This also made Prince Siddhartha very sad.

“I did not know that people die,” he said.

Prince Siddhartha went sadly back to the palace.
He could not stop thinking about the sad people he had seen.

“Why is life so sad?” said Siddhartha.
“How can people feel at peace?
I must find a way to help.
I must think very hard.”

One night Siddhartha crept out of the palace.
He was sorry to leave but he had to sort out the muddle in his head.

Siddhartha lived in the woods.

He wore rags and did not eat much.

But he went on thinking...

day after day...

year after year.

One day Siddhartha was sitting
under a Bodhi tree.
Suddenly his mind was clear.
“I know how to feel at peace,” he said.

Siddhartha began to teach people how to feel at peace.

He began to tell them stories.

He gave them rules to follow.

Many, many people heard his
stories and his rules.
They loved the things he said.
They called him The Buddha.

The Buddha lived hundreds of
years ago.
But people still tell his stories and
follow his rules.